LET'S LEARN ABOUT

MATTER

CHEMICAL
CHANGES

Rebecca Kraft Rector

Enslow Publishing
101 W. 23rd Street
Suite 240
New York, NY 10011
USA
enslow.com

WORDS TO KNOW

atom A tiny bit of matter.

chemical Having to do with chemistry.

chemistry The science that deals with properties of matter and how it forms and changes.

gas A kind of matter that has no permanent shape, like air.

liquid A kind of matter that can move freely, like water.

physical Having to do with being able to be touched or seen.

properties The qualities or features of something.

solid A kind of matter that is firm and keeps its shape.

CONTENTS

You need a very strong microscope to be able to see atoms.

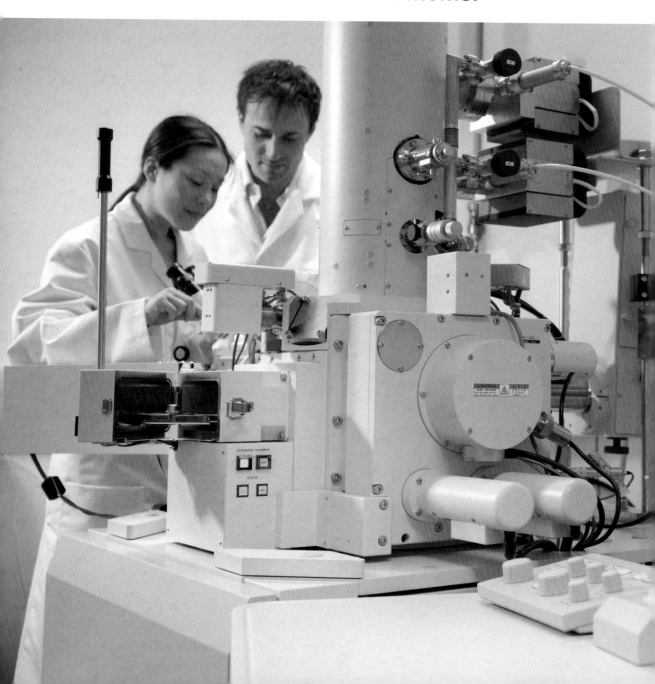

What Is Matter?

Matter is everything around you. All things are made of matter. Tiny bits of matter are called atoms. Atoms join together to make molecules.

FAST FACT

Even people are made of matter.

Matter can be a
solid, gas, or liquid.

Gas

Solid

Liquid

Common Forms of Matter

Matter has different forms. Matter can be solid. A book is a solid. Matter can be liquid. Milk is a liquid. Matter can be a gas. Oxygen is a gas.

FAST FACT

Atoms are packed tightly together in a solid.

The fork on the left has tarnished. This is a chemical change.

Properties of Matter

Properties tell about matter.
Physical properties tell how it acts,
looks, and feels. Is it big or small?
Hard or soft? Chemical properties
let matter change. An example is
being able to rust.

Cooking an egg causes a chemical change.

Changes in Matter

Matter can change. Changes can happen naturally. People can also make matter change. Matter can change in two ways. Physical change is one way. Chemical change is the other.

Creating a clay bowl is a physical change. Only the shape of the clay has changed.

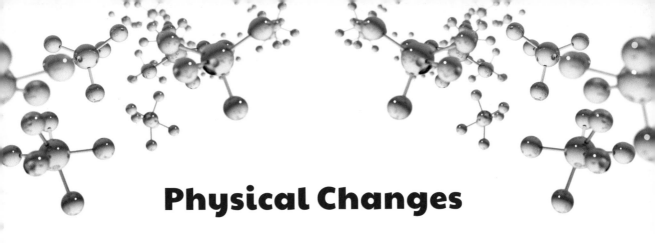

Physical Changes

Matter can make a physical change. A plate breaks. It looks different. The pieces are smaller. They are different shapes. But they are still made of the same material.

FAST FACT

Physical changes can often be changed back.

A chemical change happens when people dye their hair.

Chemical Changes

Matter can make a chemical change. Dough bakes. It changes into bread. The atoms are joined in a different way. A new material is formed.

FAST FACT

Usually you cannot undo a chemical change.

Mixing baking soda and vinegar can make a model volcano "explode."

Making a Chemical Change

Mixing can make chemical changes. Cement powder and water mix. They make a new material. It is concrete. Heating can make chemical changes. Burning wood makes a new material. It is ash.

FAST FACT

Cooking food usually makes a chemical change.

Sometimes a solid is formed during a chemical change

Light! Color! Bubbles!

Chemical changes are not always easy to see. There are clues. Watch for light. Watch for heat. Watch for a new color. Watch for a smell. Watch for bubbles.

FAST FACT

Burning wood makes heat, light, and a smell.

A volcano erupts
because of a chemical
change under the earth.

Chemical Changes Are Everywhere

Leaves change color. Wood burns. Cars rust. Bananas rot. Flowers die. These are all chemical changes. New materials have formed. The materials cannot change back.

FAST FACT

Nature makes many chemical changes.

Activity
Change for a Penny

Make your penny change color!

MATERIALS

Paper towel
Dish
Vinegar
Penny

Procedure:

Step 1: Place the folded paper towel in the dish.

Step 2: Put the penny on the paper towel.

Step 3: Pour vinegar over the penny and soak the towel.

Step 4: Leave it for a day or more.

The penny turns green! It's a chemical

change. There is copper in the penny. There is oxygen in the air. Together they form a new material. It is called copper oxide.

This copper penny turned green over time. You can make a penny turn green in one day!

Learn More

Books

Claybourne, Anna. *Make It Change!* Chicago, IL: Raintree, 2015.

Muhn, Joo-yeong. *Why Is It Rusty?* Minneapolis, MN: Big & Small, 2017.

Troupe, Thomas Kingsley. *Why Do Dead Fish Float? Learning About Matter with the Garbage Gang.* North Mankato, MN: Picture Window Books, 2015.

Websites

Scholastic
studyjams.scholastic.com / studyjams / jams / science / matter / changes-of-matter.htm
Watch this fun video and discover more about changes in matter.

Science Kids
www.sciencekids.co.nz / gamesactivities / reversiblechanges.html
Learn more about changes in matter with these fun games.

Index

Published in 2020 by Enslow Publishing, LLC.
101 W. 23rd Street, Suite 240, New York, NY 10011

Copyright © 2020 by Enslow Publishing, LLC.

All rights reserved.

No part of this book may be reproduced by any means without the written permission of the publisher.

Library of Congress Cataloging-in-Publication Data

Names: Rector, Rebecca Kraft, author.
Title: Chemical changes / Rebecca Kraft Rector.
Description: New York : Enslow Publishing, 2020. | Series: Let's learn about matter | Audience: K to grade 4. | Includes bibliographical references and index.
Identifiers: LCCN 2018045961| ISBN 9781978507579 (library bound) | ISBN 9781978509016 (pbk.) | ISBN 9781978509023 (6 pack)
Subjects: LCSH: Chemical reactions—Juvenile literature. | Matter—Properties—Juvenile literature.
Classification: LCC QD501 .R395 2020 | DDC 541/.39—dc23

LC record available at https://lccn.loc.gov/2018045961

Printed in the United States of America

To Our Readers: We have done our best to make sure all website addresses in this book were active and appropriate when we went to press. However, the author and the publisher have no control over and assume no liability for the material available on those websites or on any websites they may link to. Any comments or suggestions can be sent by e-mail to customerservice@enslow.com.

Photo Credits: Cover, p. 1 YuliaKotina/Shutterstock.com; p. 4 Monty Rakusen/Cultura/Getty Images; p. 6 Designua/Shutterstock.com; p. 8 Dmytro Yashchuk/Shutterstock.com; p. 10 Tossapol/Shutterstock.com; p. 12 tataev_foto/Shutterstock.com; p. 14 Africa Studio/Shutterstock.com; p. 16 © iStockphoto.com/Marilyn Nieves; p. 18 NatalieIme/Shutterstock.com; p. 20 beboy/Shutterstock.com; p. 23 Vincent K Ho/Shutterstock.com; interior design elements (beaker) GraphicsRF/Shutterstock.com, (molecules) 123dartist/Shutterstock.com.